UNTITLED

ACT OF GOD/ACT OF MAN

DION GREEN

WestBow Press books may be ordered through booksellers or by contacting:

WestBow Press
A Division of Thomas Nelson & Zondervan
1663 Liberty Drive
Bloomington, IN 47403
www.westbowpress.com
1 (866) 928-1240

ISBN: 978-1-9736-9127-3 (sc)
ISBN: 978-1-9736-9128-0 (e)

Library of Congress Control Number: 2020908982

Print information available on the last page.

WestBow Press rev. date: 05/15/2020

WESTBOW
PRESS®
A DIVISION OF THOMAS NELSON
& ZONDERVAN

CONTENTS

CHAPTER 1

WHAT MADE ME THE MAN I AM TODAY

Hello, my name is Dion Green. I am thirty-seven years old, and I have one daughter who is eleven years old. I would like to share with you a brief history of my past and what made me the man I am today.

I was born in the small city of Springfield, Ohio, to my mother, Denise Green, and my father, Derrick Fudge, on August 28, 1982, in a hospital that is no longer in Springfield. At the time, it was called Community Hospital, and my mother worked there for nearly twenty years of my life before retiring.

I was raised in a household with nothing but females: my mother, has three sisters, and Mom's mother, who passed in December 2017 due to breast cancer. That was a blow that devastated the family because she was the rock of the family and the backbone for all of us.

While growing up, I was always the smallest in the group but the baddest one among my friends. I remember when my friends' parents would go out of town, and we would take the car and drive around the neighborhood, though we would never go on any main street. I was usually the one driving us around. I can't even remember how I saw over the steering wheel, but I was the driver and a good one at that.

I and the other kids would go through the J. C. Penney catalogue and look at stereo stuff for a car. We said we would get this when we all came up with the money to buy a car together.

We were typical kids, growing up, being bad, and experiencing life. We went to school together and played on the same football, basketball, and baseball teams. All of us were talented in some of the sports or all of them, so that was our outlet to showcase our talents and get know in the community, especially when we played for the little league football team, the Springfield Little Tigers. A lot of athletes came from that team before going on to high school, college, and even the NFL.

While we getting older, getting more involved with sports, and starting to like girls, some of us grew apart from playing from little league. Some families moved away, and we started going to different schools in middle school and high school. In Springfield back then, there were two high schools, Springfield North and South High School. Those used to be the days because of the rivalry, but now both school have combined and taken away the rivalry that existed for decades.

When I left little league, my mom separated me from all my teammates and made me go to the opposite school of them because she didn't want me getting into trouble with my friends. All the middle schools I went to were below average when it came to the sports department.

My teammates and role model, Coach Ralph Williams, were at Hayward Middle School, but I was not allowed to go there. I was only three minutes away from the school, but my mother did not allow me to attend because all my friends went there.

I went from a winning pedigree to being on a losing team throughout my middle-school experience. I did not liking being on a losing team, especially after coming from winning championships in sport events.

While playing sports, I didn't get my growth spurt yet. It was discouraging at times, but it never got to me because in my heart, I was a lion; anyone who played with me would tell you that. Those memories would easily disappear because I always showed up when it was time.

During my last year in middle school, I knew I was about to be reunited with all my teammates in high school. But my mother sent me to Springfield North. Don't get me wrong, North was a great school. However, they could not beat South in anything while I was growing up.

Springfield South was on the south side of Springfield, mostly where all the black people grew up. Springfield North was on the north side with predominantly all white people, so there was a racial barrier there, but North did not treat anybody differently.

I attended North for three years. In my senior year, I transferred to South, but the rosters were pretty much set. I came over and had a good camp, but players who been there would cry about me getting more playing time, and the coaches would pull me out. I got angry and said, "Forget this."

I started hanging out more and didn't focus on football like I usually did. I started meeting people who sold drugs and had nice things, and it piqued my interest. Soon I started selling drugs to make money so I could buy stuff to be more self-sufficient and have money in my pocket.

Like I am with anything I put my mind into, I tried to become the best at it. I started investing more time into selling drugs, saving money, and I spent less time playing sports. I ended up having a lot of money and could buy anything I wanted, so I said goodbye to sports.

I graduated from high school in the year 2000 from Springfield South High School. I got a condo in Columbus, Ohio, which was forty minutes away from Springfield. I made the transition and started making even more money than I could imagine as a young man.

However, I always stayed humble and grateful for whatever I had. I had never been the flashy type, but I would go all out sometimes, and I would buy whatever I wanted like it was not a problem.

In that life, one minute you can have it all, and in seconds it is gone with a snap of the fingers. Therefore, I always tried to be smart with my money that I'd made risking my life and freedom every day.

All good things come to a end, and that was what happened. Someone got caught up with the wrong person, and that person told on everyone and had the cops and the Drug Enforcement Agency sent to my house, where they found large quantities of drugs and money.

In a second, I was sitting in jail on a million-dollar bond replaying my life. What had I gotten myself into? I had never been stupid; I knew every action came with consequences, so I was prepared to face whatever was given to me.

The outcome of that situation landed me in prison for seven years of my life as a young man. My daughter's mother was three months pregnant, and as I talked to God: "I know I messed up, and I accept your consequences that you will throw at me. But I'm in prison, and this was not even my mistake, so why did you hit me with the consequences and take me away from my family, where I'll have to miss the young years of my daughter's life." God never answered me.

While incarcerated, over the years I started losing all my friends to violence and illness. It was hard because I was not there to support there family through their time of need. That beat down on me.

God will never reveal his plans to you, so I was in simply in the dark through my whole time in prison. I stayed positive and took that time to get closer with God so when I came home, I could be the man he wanted me to be. I also wanted to be the father that I was supposed to be for my daughter.

While in prison, I realized God had sat me down for a reason, because I might have been going further down the wrong path where I could not be here writing to you. You know how people say, "I wish I could go back in time and change how certain things were"? That was not me because God had this plan for me.

In 2015, I was finally released from prison and was back home with my family, where I needed to be. I came home from prison and enrolled in school. In October 2018, I finished my bachelor's in science, and I am currently eight classes away from finishing my master's in business administration.

CHAPTER 2

❦

THE "ACT OF GOD" TORNADOES

My goal was to start classes back up in the summer of 2019. Everything was going as planned in life. We kicked off the summer with a Memorial Day cookout with lots of family and friends; we always did our cookout the day before Memorial Day due to family and friends having to work the following day.

To make sure things went right, I went to Kroger to buy a bigger and better grill so we could cooked all the food properly and faster. I bought the grill and had my dad put it together because I didn't have the patience to do it. Once we got it up and running, we got the food seasoned and were ready for the festivities to begin.

The whole day was filled with music, card games, and grown-up stuff like liquor and speaking about sports and life. The kids ran around having fun and sneaking in the cooler for soda and juice.

To me, this was what a cookout was about: enjoying families and friends and reminiscing on the good times we've had. As the cookout slowly approached the end, most of the adults started cleaning up all the trash lying around and got everything put up so people could leave my house. It was another successful gathering that turned out nice, and the whole day was beautiful and warm outside, so I was satisfied with the outcome.

I didn't know the following day would be filled with terror from a natural disaster that ravaged the whole community. On the actual holiday, I was at the house resting because we had had fun the day before. Throughout the day, it was beautiful and hot outside. The sun shone, and the heat was at its peak temperature. Around 9:00 p.m., the weather changed, and it became cloudy and raining outside with constant thunder and lightning.

In Ohio, we are used to rain and lightning, but this was a different type of thunderstorm. It was something I have never experienced before. The rain would pick up, and the winds would blow hard up against the house, but in my mind, this was just the weather doing what it did in Ohio.

In Ohio, especially in the Dayton area, we don't get natural disasters, so I continued to watch my television until my satellite kept losing signal. I eventually got up off the bed and monitored outside to see the rain that was passing through and making my satellite go out every thirty seconds.

I continued to monitor the storm and noticed the sky was lighting up like the Fourth of July every three seconds. Then the rain turned to golf ball–size hail, and the winds got stronger and stronger.

After noticing the change in the rain and winds, I gathered up my daughter and her mother and told them not to lie down. They should put shoes on because things did not look right to me.

Then my instincts told me to start heading to the basement, and as soon we entered the room in the basement, the noise picked up and got stronger around the house. After making sure we are all secured, I didn't see my dog, a two-year-old old American bully named Prince.

I headed back upstairs to get him, but he would not move, so I picked him up and carried him down the stairs. When I got to the last stair, the electricity shut off. I rushed to the room where my family was and closed the door.

Seconds later, I heard glass shattering, and my ear pressure got real tight while sounding like an airplane was taking off inside my house, shaking and rattling the whole building. In my mind, I still did not realize what was going on; I simply thought it is a bad windstorm.

But while my family huddled in the corner of the room, I hovered over the both of them, praying that if anything fell on my back, I could hold it up a little in case they needed to crawl out from under me to be safe.

The winds and the airplane noise stop, and the next thing I heard was my neighbor yelling my name. "Dion, are you all right?"

I replied, "Yes. Are you all right?" He said yes.

As I made my way upstairs, I saw that all my windows' glass and the material things in the house were all over the place. I made my way to the front door to check on my neighbors. As I tried to exit to the front door, it was completely pitch-black inside, so I used my light from my cell phone to guide myself through the house. I went outside to see what had happened and what damages had occurred.

As I made it to the porch, I could see only as far as my cell phone light would allow. I walked to my driveway, shone it where my cars were parked, and noticed my roof was lying on the top and the side of my cars. There was also a huge tree in the center of the street that restricted access to first responders.

My neighbor and I immediately started moving the tree with our vehicles, which were already deemed a total loss. We were wrapping the tree limbs up with chains tied to the vehicles, breaking the large parts of the tree, so first responders could get down the street to check on the rest of the neighborhood.

While we were outside trying to clear entrance for the first responders, the police officers in the neighborhood started yelling, "Get back inside! There is another tornado heading this way!" We all went back inside to our safe zone and sat there.

While we were back in the corner, I hovered over my daughter and her mother again. I started thinking to myself, *I am about to die from a tornado.* I started getting a little emotional, but I had to be strong for them. In reality, I was scared.

Twenty minutes went by, and we started to make our way back outside to resume cleaning as much as we could to help any government vehicles gain access to the street. We finally made a path for vehicles to get down the street, which was great in case someone needed medical attention.

After we got that cleared up, my neighbor and I did our own check on other people on our street to make sure they were fine. We were in shock because we did not get these types of disasters in Dayton, Ohio.

I started cleaning as much as I could. There was stuff in my yard and in my house that didn't even belong to me, so I did as much as I could until I got tired. I decided to go to sleep for a couple hours until sunrise, but I knew when the sun hit, the area was going to be in more shock then we were in now.

I woke up after a couple hours of sleep, and when I say when I stepped outside, it looked like a warzone. The homes and businesses were torn down or barely hanging on by the grace of God. Trees were everywhere in the streets and in people houses. It was a scary view for all of us because we had never seen something like this other than in movies.

The process began, and I called it Operation Cleanup. This process was awful because we had no water or electricity due to all the power lines being ripped out the ground, and the water system was down due to no electricity.

The process has to get done regardless, so I sent my daughter and fiancée to her parents until I felt like the house was ready for them to come back up and stay. My dog and I stuck it out and stayed at the house with no while I attended to rebuilding my house.

I had to start immediately because I'd let my homeowner insurance go; I was in the process of looking for a better company to insure my home, but I was too late because the tornado had come and left. All of the rebuilding was out-of-pocket expenses that I had no choice but to do in order to get my house back together and my family back home.

So while staying in the house with no power, Donita would come up after work to bring me food and water for the evening so I could make it through the night. But that was when the power of God stepped in an helped out. The City of Dayton stood so strong when the disaster occurred, and people started showing up with ice, food, water, and toiletries to make sure we were all right. This was an everyday process for weeks.

That was where the phrase "Dayton Strong" came from because the community was amazing. They were there for us twenty-four seven throughout the days, weeks, and months while we faced this tough time. The Memorial Day Tornadoes became the name of the eighteen tornadoes that hit Dayton, Ohio.

Through devastation came unity for the most part, because we were helping each other out in the neighborhood every day to help clean or remove stuff from properties; it was too much for one or two people. It was an overwhelming experience, and we all were exhausted by time the sun set after cleaning up for hours in scorching heat.

While cleaning my property, I had a massive tree that came out of the ground and crushed everything it landed on. The three was to the left of me and on my neighbor's property. There was a school across the street, and two thirty-five-feet steel beams landed on my property, taking out my roof and planting themselves in the house, taking out the cables line and crushing my neighbor's car. The other one landed in the back of the house, straddling the fence between me and my neighbor. It was amazing seeing how this had made it over to my house, but thankfully it did not rip the house in two.

But enough of seeing what could have happened—it was time to get back to work and haul stuff away from the property. We worked from sunrise to sunset every day. The phrase I used was Groundhog Day, from the movie, because it seemed like I was cleaning the same area. The days were starting to feel like the previous ones.

Things were starting to get better. A lot of people would come around and offer help in cleaning up and cutting trees so the debris could be removed from properties. I ordered my windows the following day, but as one can imagine, windows were on back order because every house needed them. Until then, I kept my window boarded up with a sheet of oriented strand boards.

I had already placed an order to get my roofing materials so I could get my house covered up correctly instead of using a blue tarp, like the whole community had been using. Our neighborhood looked like the Smurfs due to blue tarps on every house.

While my daughter was staying in Springfield, Ohio, she told her mom that she did not want to come back home because of the tornadoes. Every year, she went to Las Vegas for the summer to spend time with her grandpa, so I had until then to get things together for her. My goal was to get things back in order before she came home on August 23, two days before her birthday.

Things were starting to look like they were getting better, and that was a relief. I wanted to redecorate an paint her room so when she got home, it would be different, and hopefully her mind would change about wanting to be here.

I had her mom pick out a theme and a color, and that was what we were going to do for her early birthday present—when she return, she'd see a whole different look. We found the color and theme, so I called my dad and told him I needed him to paint Niara's room before August 23.

Deep down, I felt relief and started to feel like myself house was coming along. Getting my daughter's room decorated before she came home felt like I was back on the right path. I felt like I was behind on everything because cleaning was a full-time job for weeks.

While I was cleaning, my buddy Steve from Springfield called me and said, "Hey, Dion, do you want to go canoeing down the river today?"

At first I said no because I thought, *Why stop doing what you are doing to go have fun when you can be using that time to get close to being done?*

However, after a while, I picked up my phone, called back, and said, "I'll meet you at the river in Springfield, Ohio, at Mad River Adventures, to go canoeing." That was the first bit of fun I'd had since the tornadoes, and I was happy I got out and enjoyed the beautiful day. We were on the river for about five hours.

After we got out of the river, instead of driving back to Dayton, I decided to go to my mother's house to shower an clean myself up. I would also get to see them because since the disaster, I had been so busy that I hadn't seen them.

CHAPTER 3

THE "ACT OF MAN" TERROR

After taking my shower and getting dressed at my mother's house, I called my dad, my sister, and my friend to let them know I was in town, so they could come by, have a couple of drinks, and chill. Everyone came by to chill, and I went to liquor store to get some Jack Daniels because my dad and I drank whiskey. I bought that, came back, sat on my mom's patio, and hung out on a nice beautiful night.

While we were drinking and feeling good, I asked my mom if she could watch my nephew so my sister and her husband could hang out with me for the night. She agreed to it. I suggested everybody get in my truck and go to my house for a little bit to have some shots and figure out what to do.

We arrived at my place. My girl was already lying in the bed, and I told her the family was here, so that I was going to take them out. "Do you wanna come?" I asked. She got up and got dressed, and we took our shots of liquor and headed to the cars. We ended up taking two cars because my girl made the car jam-packed. We made our way down to the Oregon District to have some fun. It was my sister's husband's birthday, so I was happy I got to take them out to enjoy the night.

As we reached the parking lot for the Oregon District, my dad was already asleep in the car, and I laughed. I told him to stay in the car because we were not going to be in there that long. At first he agreed to it, but then he said, "Dion, you going in?" I said yes. He replied, "Then I am too."

I said, "Come on, then."

We walked toward the club, Ned Peppers. I normally came to this club in the Oregon District, but when it was our turn to get in, they said we could not go because my dad had on sweatpants. We said, "Forget it. Let's go to the other club, Newcom Tavern." It was right across the street from the Ned Peppers.

We entered the club and headed upstairs to the bar to order drinks. Usually I ordered all the drinks, but my dad said, "I've got it. Don't worry about it." I said okay. I enjoyed my night, and my sister and her husband enjoyed each other's company. My dad was out there dancing all over the place and having a good time, and that was all that mattered.

Donita and I stood against the bar, talking an watching them enjoy themselves. My dad came over an ordered me and her another drink. He was being overprotective, saying things like, "Why is that guy staring? Is it at you or your girl?"

I said, "Dad, I've got this if he approaches her."

While the drinks came, security walked over. "Sir, your dad has been dancing inappropriately."

I replied, "Uh, okay, we're leaving." I told everyone to go.

We exited the club, and everybody was with us except my sister and her husband. We waited at the taco stand for them to come out, but there was no sign of them. I looked again but didn't see them, so I came back out to stand with my dad and my girl, and I sent another friend in there to look for them.

That moment, while waiting on my sister, her husband, and my friend to come back out the club, became the worst day of my life and the last moments I would get to share with my father.

While waiting on them to come back out the club, on the side of the club, a tall, slender white guy had a mask covering half his face, and his body was covered in body armor. He came down the side of the building and fired numerous gunshots in our direction. Afterward, he walked through where we was lying on the ground and stepped over Donita to cross the street.

I was in disbelief of this shooting—the Oregon District is a heavily guarded area with a lot of police officers in the vicinity. In my mind, I thought the guy was drunk and being stupid. I thought as soon as the police saw him, they would arrest him for causing panic in the area.

But it was not no joke, and it was so real when he stepped over Donita to cross the street to Ned Pepper's. We heard gunshots being fired like someone was letting off a whole roll of firecrackers in the area. Once he starting opening fire, the crowd panicked, and everybody was running and trying to take cover so they would not get hit.

While he caused panic on the other side of the street, Donita got up from playing possum on the ground to find my sister and her husband. I was still there with my father in between the cars, telling him to get up because we were getting out of here. He kept lying there, and I said, "Come on, let's go."

While I was talking to my dad, there was another person on the sidewalk in front of me at the taco stand, asking me to call the ambulance because the person had been shot. I thought, Really? This is real? I am now calling 911 for this person in front of me to get help. The phone kept ringing, probably due to everyone calling about the situation at hand.

While trying to get an answer on the phone with the police, I went back to my father and told him to get up. I looked at his body and didn't see any gunshot wounds at first. "Come on, Dad. Let's!" He kept looking steadily at me.

I flipped the flashlight feature on my phone to look at his body and once again didn't see blood or any signs of bullets. Then I got closer to his head and shined my light around his head and shoulders area. As I leaned down toward his head, I notice a puddle of blood around his head. I started to panic because I was lost and did not understand.

As I spoke to my dad, he kept lying there with his eyes open, also gasping for air. I started screaming for help over and over.

While performing CPR, I kept yelling for help. I stopped performing CPR and wrapped my arms around my dad, telling him, "You're okay. Get up. I love you." That was all I wanted him to hear from me until he left me. His eyes were still open while looking at me, like he wanted to say something, but he never did.

The paramedics came and asked if I could move so they could assist my father, but I knew it was too late. I clung to my dad as if I was a boa constrictor refusing to let go of his prey. Police and medics tried to move me off of him, and they finally got me up and walked me to the corner while they performed their duties.

MIKE DeWINE
GOVERNOR

September 12, 2019

Dion Green
120 W. Mullberry St.
Springfield, OH 45506

Dear Dion,

On August 4th, I ordered all the flags in the state to be flown at half-staff to honor and remember the victims from the Oregon District shooting that morning.

Enclosed is one of those flags that flew over the Ohio Statehouse. Please accept this flag from Fran and me and all the citizens of the State of Ohio.

We will never forget Derrick.

Very respectfully yours,

Mike DeWine
Ohio Governor

STATE OF OHIO
HOUSE OF REPRESENTATIVES

IN MEMORY OF DERRICK RAMON FUDGE

We were deeply saddened to learn of the death of Derrick Ramon Fudge and extend our sincere condolences to his family and friends.

Derrick Fudge left an indelible impression on the people whose lives he touched, and he will be remembered as a spirited individual who contributed immeasurably to the world around him. His concern for improving the quality of life in our society was clearly evident in his personal sacrifices of time and energy to his family, friends, and community, and his absence will be keenly felt.

Thriving in the circle of his loved ones, including his son, Dion, his granddaughter, Niara, and his siblings, Sherrie, Twyla, Roderick, Leonard, and Jeffrey, Derrick Fudge always used his talents to the benefit of those around him, and the laurels of his life stand as a tribute not only to him but also to those he left behind. Although the void his death has created can never be filled, the legacy of care and commitment he established will surely live on. It is certain that the world is a richer place for his having been in it, and he will be sorely missed.

Thus, with heartfelt sympathy, we mourn the loss and salute the memory of a truly unique man, Derrick Ramon Fudge.

Representative Fred Strahorn
House District 39

Representative Kyle Koehler
House District 79

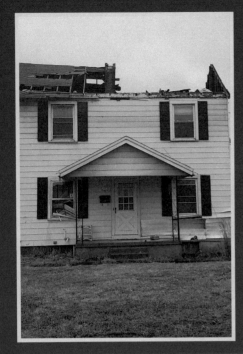

Now I was in an all-out rage because I knew I'd just lost my father. When I saw them place a white sheet over my dad's body, I lost it. I broke loose from the police, ran over to my dad, and dropped to the ground. I started punching the concrete while screaming and yelling, "Why?"

Family and officers tried to console me, but I didn't want to be touched. I wanted to be left alone at the time. While in anger and crying, I had an out-of-body experience.

The police officers came up to me and said, "We need to escort you to where the Dub Pub is at, to speak to the detectives." While walking to the Dub Pub, I saw bodies lying on the sidewalk covered up in white sheets, and blood was everywhere on the pavement.

It was so upsetting because this was a nightmare of terror that I was looking at while making my way to the bus to sit and wait until it was time to speak to detectives. After getting on the bus, I was all right until my emotions and anger took over again. Then I started punching the windows and screaming in an all-out rage.

So they pulled me off the bus, sat me down on the pavement, and gave me water. People were trying to offer comfort, but I was stretch out across the pavement with my head down, crying the whole time until they picked me up and took me inside to speak with the detectives. There, I tried to answer questions to help with the investigation.

I was so lost an confused that I was not any help at the time. All I could say was I'd seen him walk down the side of the building in black with a half face mask and a gun.

They release me and Donita, and we were able to go home. I was told I had lost my mind again because I believed there was another shooter and that they were coming for my family. I hid in the bushes at home, waiting for any car that did not belong on the street. I was ready to jump out and protect my family from any more harm.

While sitting in the bushes, my neighbors and family were pleading with me to come out, but I would not come out because I felt like we were still in danger. Eventually I came into the house and turned on the news to see what really was happening.

While turning on the news, I found out that the shooter's name was Connor Betts and that he'd killed nine people, including himself, an injured multiple people while attempting to kill his sister, Megan Betts, who was his intended target.

While I was at home with family, the detectives came by for a visit to check on me and see whether I could be better help on what had happened that night. While we sat inside my house, they asked me numerous questions. "Do you remember speaking to any girl that night?" I said, "No, why would I? Donita was with me, and my father was just shot, so where would I find the time to speak to anybody?" They did not ask me that question anymore.

While I sat with my family and grieved, my cousin pulled up a picture off of Facebook of his sister, and I said, "That was the person who asked me for help and said to call the ambulance, because she said she had been shot." Initially, when she asked, I thought it was a male asking me, but while my mind and thoughts came back, I saw why the detectives had asked me that question about speaking to a female.

The next day, when the officers came back over, I told them yes, but I thought it was a male. They said, "We knew you did, but your mind was still trying to process it all."

That was when they told me that she was the intended target. "You and your family just happened to be at the taco stand where this horrible event took place." I broke down in tears again, saying, "Why me? I was just in the tornadoes, and now this. I am confused about life right now. Why is all this happening to me in a short span of time?"

Family and friends kept saying that my dad was there to protect me from harm, and he gave his life for me to carry on with my life, continue raising my daughter, and become something greater in life that God has in store for me.

While they are telling me this, in my mind, I ask God, *Why have you put so much weight and burden on my shoulders? Why have you put me through so much?*

People kept saying to me that God didn't place anything on me that I could not handle. They were speaking the truth, but at the time, I did not hear any of that.

I was already questioning my faith because I still had no understanding about why this happened to me. I was angry with him, But deep down, I knew God did not make mistakes and that he had a plan for all of us. This was written to happen before I and my dad were conceived on this earth.

I knew that this was meant to me, but as a human with emotions, it was a natural feeling to have at the moment. If I hadn't questioned my faith, I would be asking myself whether there was something wrong with me.

A couple days went by. The shooting become nationwide news because hours prior to the shooting in Dayton, another had occurred in El Paso, Texas, claiming twenty-two innocent lives at a local Walmart store.

Throughout the week of getting prepared for my father's funeral, the news media was everywhere in Dayton, reporting on the story, showing up at families' houses, and trying to get in contact with all of us. At first I was against doing an interview and talking about the nightmare that had claimed lives due to a senseless act of gun violence.

But during the night, something happened to me and told me to do an interview and speak about who my father was and what he loved to do. I therefore contacted some of the reporters and said I would speak about it as much as I could.

It was hard speaking about the topic, but in some way it was a form of therapy to talk about it and release some stress building inside of me. We all grieve differently. Some hide, and others speak about it to help them get through the storm. My choice was to talk about it.

Chapter 4

Coming to Terms That This Was Real

That was the hardest week of my life because it was on every news nation and radio station across the country. Every time I saw my dad's picture or heard his name, I broke down and cried.

The love and support I had around me was amazing. Every time I got angry or upset, God would send someone in my directions to help me calm down and get me back to feeling all right. He placed so many great people around me that helped me get through the week. My victim advocate, Tara Poteet, was so helpful through every step of the process. She would call and check on me, telling me things I could do. I would text or call her every day and tell her how grateful I was to have her assigned to me as my advocate, because she would go above and beyond for me. It was comforting to know that a person I had just become acquainted with had so much compassion for me. I am thankful for you, Tara.

Also, my executive director, Michael Vanderburg, played a major part every step of the way. I remember getting a text from my supervisor from work saying his boss would like to have my number. I told him it was fine to forward my information to Michael, and as soon as I spoke to Michael, he showed up at the house in less than twenty minutes.

Michael has been sent to me from God to help me get back on the right track and not to let my emotions take me off the path of righteousness, I can be having a bad day and call Michael, and he will give me advice or come over at the drop of a hat. He always reassures me, "Dion, you will rise and become something greater than what you are now. You will have an impact in this world."

Hearing that makes me say, "Why me?" But like I said, you never know what God has planned for your life, because to have an impact on a world, you have to go through it yourself and understand the pain and suffering other people are experiencing.

While we were sitting on the front porch of my house and talking among each other, an older white gentlemen pulled up and said, "Hey, I used to live in your house."

At first I was leery about this guy, and I thought he was with the media, trying to be nosy about the situation. I rose off the porch and walked toward his pickup truck to listen to what he had to say. When I looked back to tell Michael, "One second," Michael was right behind me. The older gentlemen and I started to converse about him living here, and he said that he used to live here twenty-five years ago.

My next question to him was, "What made you drive by today and tell me that you live here?" I found out he was a veteran, and his wife had died. He wanted to ride through his old neighborhood and reminisce on things. I was still kinda of leery until he start speaking about my neighbor, so I knocked on my neighbor's door and ask, "Do you know him?" I found out he was telling the truth.

After I connected them with each other to catch up with each other, I told Michael, "Let's go inside the house and finish our conversation." However, about fifteen minutes later, my fiancée came into the kitchen and said there was a older guy at the door.

I went to the door to greet him, and he said, "Do you mind if I can see how you remodeled the house?" I said sure, and I took him through and showed him the changes I'd made. He was amazed.

I finished showing him the house, and we stopped in the kitchen. Then he started crying an apologizing for not knowing what had just happened to me. He said he'd lost his wife, and it had been a hard and long process to overcome. I gave him a hug and said, "You are all right with me." He was simply a lonely guy out driving.

The moral of me sharing this story is that God was already starting to work through me to help console people whose hearts were torn due to losing someone in their lives. I could have gotten angry because I was grieving, but here came someone sharing his emotions with me. God had sent him to me for a reason.

After he left, Michael and I finished our conversation, and then Michael left. I tried to lie down to get some rest, but I could not sleep or eat. I think I was scared to go to sleep and wake up to realize that this was a real situation I was dealing with. I didn't want to face reality.

I shut off all the TVs in the house and turned off my phone so I could try to pull myself together. The television was constantly showing the shooting, and my phone would not stop ringing from family and friends calling to check on me.

On top of that, planning the funeral was the hardest thing to do in my life. We were having a good time enjoying the night with family, and now I had to pick out a suit for my father's homecoming. Preparation was unreal.

Throughout the whole week, my family was surrounding me to make sure that I was all right, because I still was not sleeping or eating. On top of that, I would break down and cry but then go to being angry at everybody. They was there to make sure I didn't cause harm to others or myself.

Because I was experiencing every emotion a human being could encounter leading up to the funeral, I placed blame on myself. If I had not called him, this would not have happened and he would still be with me now.

I kept reliving the whole night of the shooter walking down the side of the building, and I had thoughts on what I could have done to prevent this from happening to all the victims who lost their lives that night.

I got mad because I kept saying that I didn't take the situation seriously enough to try to do something until it was too late. That bothered me because I was too late to respond to anything; I was in shock and had not believed it was happening, but it was very real.

I give our first responders great praise for the fast response they had to contain the shooter and take him down in thirty seconds at Ned Peppers. I was happy he was contained in a fast manner, but I was angry he was shot and killed. However, it had to be done, or else many more lives would have been taken.

The reason I was upset about the outcome was because he took the easy way out, instead of learning the lives of each victim, finding out about each individual, and seeing the suffering and pain that families and friends of the victims were going through. But he was on a suicide mission, and he would never get the chance to find out. I am going to share each victim's stories and keep their legacy alive as much I can for them and their families.

The funeral was approaching, and it was time to make arrangements and get the program in order. I left the funeral arrangement to my uncle Jeff, my dad's youngest brother, and I would okay it. The only thing I told him was that I would pick the suit and get Dad's appearance together for the funeral. I made my way down to Price Store in downtown Dayton to find my father a suit to wear so I could send him home looking good.

I decided on a black suit with a red tie and handkerchief. It was sharp to me, and I could visualize my dad in the suit. I gave them my dad's sizes, and they told me to come back the next day to pick it up. His attire was completed.

The next day, the funeral home called me and asked if I could bring them the suit my dad was wearing, so they could dress him up. I went to the store to pick it up, and the owner of the store gave me the suit for my father for free. That was very nice, and I hugged him and started crying, saying, "Thank you very much for doing this."

I had the suit in my car, ready to be transported to the funeral home, where my dad body was. I was up in the air about taking it down to Springfield because I did not want to go there or even walk inside the funeral home, knowing my dad was in there and was not leaving with me. It was a very hard moment, and I asked God for strength the whole ride to the funeral home. I got it done and left, but all of sudden, I broke down and cried the whole trip back home on the highway.

I never knew that in death, so many things were required to make sure a funeral was right and properly done. While getting all that in order, I still had to take care of all his legal actions and affairs. This was a new area for me, but I had no choice. I had to learn and learn quick, but I got it all together an taken care of.

While doing that last little bit of stuff and running to make sure everything was taken care of for the funeral tomorrow, I tried to not think about tomorrow. I had some family over. We drank my dad's drink, Jack Daniels; listened to music; and tried to not think what was upon us.

I already told myself I was not going to sleep because I didn't want to go to sleep, wake up, and find it was a new day that I did not want to see. But what the body wants, the body will get, so I ended up falling asleep. Mind you, I still wasn't sleeping or eating prior to this, so my body took over and shut me down for several hours.

CHAPTER 5

THE HARDEST PART IN MY LIFE

Here it was, the day I was dreading: funeral day. My phone rang, and people in the house were getting dressed. I lay there not wanting to get out of bed, get dressed, or move. I dragged my feet the whole time.

Eventually, I got up, washed my face an brushed my teeth, and looked in the mirror. I screamed "Why me?" There was no answer, so I got dressed and got everyone out of the house. We loaded up in the cars to make our way down to Springfield to my uncle Jeff's house, where the family would meet up.

On the highway ride to Springfield, I looked out the window, wishing the ride was from Dayton to California, but it was only a thirty-minute drive. We made our way to my uncle's house, and everybody looked very nice for the celebration that was about to take place.

As we piled into the limos and headed over to St. John Church, where the service was being held, I saw nothing but love throughout the place and outside.

We exited the vehicle and lined up to start making our way inside the church. My dad was at the front of the church in a beautiful casket, and I could see some of him in his suit. While walking up to the casket, I prayed for the strength that I could do it. God granted me the strength to make it there.

I knew this was the last time I would see my dad, so I got up there, got weak, and broke down. I started crying and saying, "We were just having fun, and now I'm saying my goodbyes." It tore me apart.

As I made it to my seat, I saw the place was filled from top to bottom with all races showing their love and support. The governor and Mrs. Dewine attended, as well as the mayor from Springfield. Dayton mayor Nan Whaley attended, and the love and support that poured out from the building was amazing. I was told there was a line wrapped around the building outside for people to come in and show their respects.

While people came to view my father, they would also come over to the family and hug us. The whole time, my eyes were closed, but I could recognize certain voices who were speaking to me. It was too hard for me to open my eyes again and see him in a casket.

My aunt did the ministry, and she did a great job, but she rubbed a lot of people the wrong way. She kept saying he was a man who had little to offer, which was disturbing. I just kept it to myself so that the service could hurry up and get done. I was ready to leave that church and get away from certain people who were around me.

I made it through the service, and as we walked my father to the car and got him settled, I broke loose from everyone, got in my own car, and left. I drove to where my real friends and family were and told them to go where the bypass was going to be, which was Casey Hall.

As we got to Casey Hall to set things up, the food was supposed to be delivered there so everyone could eat. Instead, they delivered it to the church. I started getting mad an frustrated because things were not going as planned.

My executive director from work, Michael Vanderburg, saw the frustration on my face and placed an order. He quickly got the situation under control and said, "Dion, don't worry about it. I promise you." Michael has been there for me when I don't even expect him to be. It is amazing how God aligns you with great people.

The food arrived, and everybody was ready to eat, but before we ate, we had to bless the food. Michael said a prayer, blessing the food, then it was time to eat up. The kids lined up first to get their plates, and the adults came second.

While people were sitting down, eating their meals, and listening to music, more and more people pulled up to the gathering, showing love and support to each other while making their way around the building.

Music played, and all the kids took over the playlist and selected the songs they wanted to hear so they could do dances they learned from watching YouTube. We adults recorded all the kids dancing and having fun on a very sad day.

While the kids were doing their thing, we adults enjoyed the moment. I had a big gallon of Jack Daniels, and I poured everyone of age a shot of liquor. Then I told everyone to raise their glasses and said, "To the remembrance of my father." I told everyone, "Thank you for your support and love." Then we saluted in the memories of my father.

I cannot lie: seeing everyone having a good time, enjoying the moment, and playing catch-up because they haven't seen each other in years had me in tears. It did not seem right that my dad was not here, being the person he was, making people laugh, and playing with the kids.

As the night approached and the gathering was nearing its end, a couple other family members started helping me pick up trash and get things back in order before we left. Family and friends were leaving and making their way around the building, giving each other hugs. It was awesome to see people share their love with each other.

I was exhausted and ready to get home and be by myself, because tomorrow we was doing the final celebration at my uncle's house with food, a DJ, and fireworks. I needed to get home and rest so I could wrap my mind around the whole situation.

I want to thank the Rocking Horse for donating the food. The Rocking Horse has been in our family for a while because my grandmother worked there for years before she passed on December 31, 2017. All the people there loved my Memaw like she was their grandmother. That was special to me because they didn't have to do that at all.

The day was here, and the festivities began with family everywhere, music blaring loud in the neighborhood, an people hanging out to celebrate my father's homecoming to be with the Lord. As the day turned into night, we set up across the street in the field and put on a fireworks show for the grand finale. It was beautiful, and he would had been proud of how we sent him off and celebrated his life.

Once the festivities were over, it was time to head home and back to reality—and the reality was I was still not sleeping. I woke up at two every night in a cold sweat. Every time I fell into a deep sleep, I went right back to the night of the shooting and seeing my dad fight for what would be his last breaths.

Finally I called my doctor, told her I could not sleep, and admitted that I needed to seek counseling as soon as possible. I was given sleeping pills to sleep, and I started speaking to a professional trauma counselor. Things were starting to feel a little better as the day progressed even though I was still mentally and emotionally tired.

Seeking help was the best thing I could had done. My counselor explained to me the symptoms I would experience from going through two tragedies less than two months apart. That was the best decision I'd made since facing those life-changing moments.

I still see her to this day because some weeks are better than others. She talks and listens to what I am experiencing and gives me certain techniques to help me get through whatever I might be facing at the time.

She told me what I have is acute post-traumatic stress disorder because I was there, and the visions were so vivid that it took me back there at the drop of a dime. My body was in hyperarousal mode, meaning that it was very tense and alert to all types of things after being in two disasters.

While I am going through my spills, I am still concerned about the well-being of others going through pain. I wrote to all the families in Odessa, Texas, and to the mother of the shooter, offering my condolences to them because in order to heal, you have to forgive.

I am trying to start my healing process, and I knew I would not be able to heal if I did not forgive and did not practice what I preach. I had to lift the anger out of my heart so I could continue to try to move forward and help others who were suffering as well.

Weeks went by. I tried to get back to work so I could get back to my regular routine. I wanted to get back to normalcy, but it was hard to return to that with the media and the Dayton Foundation speaking about the money each member of the victim would get.

Like I said to them via e-mail, I thanked them for what they had done for us. But when money gets involved, it becomes another nightmare due to greed and everyone wanting some type of exchange for who they are to the victims.

What they don't understand is money is only a temporary relief, but it will never bring back my father or erase visions I have from watching my dad take his last breath in front of me while lying on the street, shot and helpless.

With that being said, I cannot wait for the money part to be over with so people and families can finally move forward and begin their true grieving process without friends and family being concerned about money or trying to figure out a way to get a part of something that doesn't even amount to the life that was taken from us.

There was another foundation, called the Connor Group, that was helping the victims' families from the Oregon shooting. I like how they operate; they keep a low profile and do not broadcast their monetary gains. They contacted us and unveiled what they had done for us.

Like I said, I appreciate everything anyone does, but how the Dayton Foundation was broadcasting over the news every day started to make me worry about the safety of my family and the other victims' families. With money involved in the situation, people will do stupid things to acquire it.

I am writing this to y'all before any money has been disbursed and before the 2019 holidays start to roll around. My father's birthday is November 1, so this is the beginning of some very emotional months that are ahead of me.

I am hoping for the best, but I also expect the worse to arise when coming to the realization that we won't hang out these holidays. I am trying to prepare myself for these days that are quickly approaching.

But what I want to say to anybody who is reading this is no matter how mad or upset you are with your loved ones, please take the time to cherish them every moment you can. I never would have thought in a million years that the night we went out was my father's last day on earth. I went from having a good time to living a nightmare.

Please tell your mom, dad, family, and friends that you loved them because we never know what the man upstairs has in store for any of us. It takes only seconds to show or tell someone how you feel.

I also want to pass on advice to the next person who is going through hard times and facing adversity. Please don't give up on yourself. It is hard—I understand. But we shall overcome any obstacle with faith and spiritual guidance.

I know times get hard, but we all face hard times. Maybe they are not as hard as the next person, but God will not place anything on us that we cannot handle, so continue to praise and worship him, and God will do the work for you.

Thanks to the special people in my life:

Dayton, Ohio, and Springfield, Ohio, for the love and support
Sally Dwyer
The Honoring Network
Victory Project's Monnin Bush
Tara Poteet, victim advocate
The Vannoy Firm and Anthony Vannoy
Dave Chappelle
Kanye West
Amy Tichler
Cheryl Dillin
Dayton Foundation
Connor Group Foundation